The New Tes… Use of the Jewish Scriptures

David Allen

Academic Dean, The Queen's Foundation, Birmingham

GROVE BOOKS LIMITED

RIDLEY HALL RD CAMBRIDGE CB3 9HU

Contents

First Impression December 2023
ISSN 1365-490X
ISBN 978 1 78827 357 2

1 Introduction

The late New Testament scholar Martin Hengel is reputed to have said, 'If all you know is the New Testament, you do not know the New Testament.' This booklet seeks—in part—to endorse Hengel's claim, and considers the use of the Jewish Scriptures within the New Testament texts. We shall suggest that, to read the New Testament well, attending to its use of, and appeal to, the Jewish Scriptures is a requisite task. That is, when interpreting a New Testament text, a good initial question to ask is, 'How are the Jewish Scriptures being used here'?

Why so? In part, it is because so much of the NT draws on the narratives and imagery of Israel's Scriptures, and such connections therefore shape how the NT is composed and interpreted. Scriptural concepts such as covenant or promise, characters such as Moses or Sarah, or themes such as exodus or exile feature prominently across the NT testimony. But it also follows from the NT writers themselves being (primarily) Jewish, and seeking to make sense of the Christ event in the light of their own scriptural testimony. Such christological reflection develops from engaging with the NT writers' (own) Scriptures and the imagery and concepts therein.

Mapping the Territory

It is generally agreed that the earliest Christian documents available to us are the letters of St Paul, with 1 Corinthians likely one of the earliest within the Pauline corpus. Particularly in the second half of the epistle, Paul is invited to offer his apostolic view on various presenting concerns, reflecting the ways in which new doctrine and practice was birthed in response to the good news of Jesus Christ (1 Cor 7.1–16.24). In so doing, Paul occasionally appeals to what he had inherited from others before him. This might reflect what Paul had learnt about Jesus (1 Cor 7.10–11; Paul not being part of the original 'Jesus movement'), but it also includes wider tradition previously received from other ecclesial sources (1 Cor 11.23). Paul was frequently defending the origins of his calling and ministry, and its direct provenance from the risen Christ (Gal 1.11–24). Hence any reference to *inheriting* tradition, to material that preceded him, is notable. It demonstrates what we might call the earliest or foundational dimensions of the gospel testimony, the fundamental kerygma or proclaimed message concerning Jesus Christ. Paul's testimony that he had received the words of institution from Jesus Christ (1 Cor 11.23–26) is one such intriguing example, but perhaps the more fundamental one in terms of early gospel proclamation is the opening declaration of 1 Corinthians 15, in which Paul recounts the pre-existing tradition that he had received in respect of the death and resurrection of Jesus Christ (1 Cor 15.3–8).

What is striking about this tradition is the twice-stated declaration that both Jesus' death and resurrection occurred *in accordance with the Scriptures* (1 Cor 15.3–4). As the early church grappled with the implications of the Christ event and with the identity of Jesus, Scripture offered the authoritative source for such reflection. Or to put it another way, making sense of the Christ event was from its very outset an OT-orientated or OT-informed exercise.[1] The Jewish Scriptures were the locus—or the 'go-to' place—for trying to make sense of Jesus. Paul mentions no explicit passages in this regard—it would have been great if he had! His non-specificity may instead point to the wider scope of the Scriptures, that the scriptural testimony *as a whole* speaks to the death and resurrection of Jesus Christ.

The NT texts' use of the Jewish Scriptures is integral to their understanding

This premise remains significant for those who read the NT as twenty-first-century readers, trying to make sense of the constituent texts and their claims about Jesus. That is, if one is to follow Paul's lead and, as we shall see, that of a number of other NT authors, the NT texts' appropriation and use of the Jewish Scriptures is integral to their understanding. Such usage might take place in various ways. It might be a formal scriptural quotation or citation, signalled by a preceding introductory formula such as 'as it is written' (1 Cor 1.19). It might be an allusion or echo to an idea or saying from the Scriptures, with a particular word or phrase bringing forth resonance to be explored. John's gospel, for example, begins 'In the beginning' (John 1.1), language that seems to allude to similar terminology in Gen 1.1, and the attentive reader is thereby encouraged by the evangelist to make wider connections to Genesis 1 and to the creation account therein. It might be a catena of passages strung together for rhetorical effect (compare Rom 3.10–18), or a more extended quotation/citation that is then expounded in homiletic fashion (Jer 31.31–34 in Heb 8.8–12). The relationship might be thematic as much as lexical. Hebrews' interest in covenant and sacrificial matters, for instance, points to a plethora of scriptural connections. It might be an appeal to a particular character from the Jewish Scriptures—Abraham or Sarah, perhaps, or Hannah or David. Or it might invoke a wider narrative of which such figures form a part—Israel's exodus, perhaps, or the offering of Isaac (Gen 22; the so-called *Akedah*) and the degree to which that might—or might not—be seen as a model of Jesus' own self-giving. It may be that such narratival invocation is more subtle or merely hinted at, but when the reader's scriptural radar is metaphorically switched on, potential resonances may be identified and forthcoming.

Take, for example, Mark's retelling of the death of John the Baptist (Mark 6.14–29). The account is longer or more developed than that of its synoptic siblings, and unusually so, as Mark lays out the details of Herodias' role in securing the death of John. The narrative can work, of course, without any reference to scriptural echoes, but it takes on further depth if / when one recalls Mark's earlier patterning of the Baptist in terms of Elijah. Such patterning has been established from the outset of Mark's account, with John's attire drawing on similar language used of Elijah (Mark 1.6; compare 2 Kgs 1.7–8). And it seems to extend to the execution of John, which has resonances with the pursuit of Elijah in 1 Kings, and particularly Jezebel's forceful role in it (rather than that of Ahab—hence the implied weakness of both male kings). The inclusion of this extra frame of reference in Mark's gospel—an account which is otherwise generally brief and rapid in its narration—testifies to its wish to reinforce the Elijah-John relationship and enable that to inform Mark's account of Jesus.

The terminology with which connections are made to the OT also varies from NT author to author and has interpretative significance in that way. Paul uses the language of 'it is written,' ascribing a textual flavour to the citation mode; Hebrews puts the scriptural language on divine lips—it is divine speech, and God, Jesus, and even the Spirit, voice Scripture. Imagery of fulfilment is common particularly in Matthew's birth narrative or John's account of Jesus' death, and this offers a particular lens onto what the respective author thinks Scripture *is* and how it is critical to understanding Jesus' life and death. Likewise, the volume of scriptural usage also varies between NT texts. The Book of Revelation famously has no direct OT quotation, but its whole tenor is full of scriptural resonance; a cursory read through Revelation 4–5 generates numerous references or echoes of the texts of Daniel or Ezekiel or Isaiah (and one can easily misunderstand Rev 4–5 if one disregards these scripturally-sourced connections). Similarly, NT authors themselves are not consistent. Paul's discourse to the Romans is frequently built around scriptural quotation, whereas the Epistle to Philippians is largely devoid of them—at least in formal terms. (But when one presses the concept more generally, it is surprising how many can be discerned).

Other interpretative questions arise. Precisely which scriptural texts are being cited? What is their provenance or form? As the Jewish Scriptures circulated in several variant forms and linguistic traditions—Hebrew, Greek, Aramaic—the particular textual choice will likely have interpretative significance. Just as in our modern

Precisely which scriptural texts are being cited? What is their provenance?

context, when a specific version of the Bible (the King James or the NIV or a paraphrase rendering such as The Message) presents a particular rendering or idea, the OT citation's precise text form may prove to be explanatorily significant. Or what happens, for example, when the cited text form seems unknown, or when the NT author seems to change it? The form of Ps 68.18 in Eph 4.8 is seemingly a reversal of that found in Psalms, and may derive from a different source or psalmic corpus. Sometimes the text just looks a bit *different* from its OT predecessor—the Song of Moses sung in Rev 15.3–4 seems to draw on Exodus association and language, and is named after Moses, but appears still to be a *new* song in that regard and different from its Exodus 15 predecessor. And then there are further debates as to what defines a text as scriptural—what makes it as such? Jude seems to quote the book of 1 Enoch (Jude 14–15) and does so attributing some form of authority or significance to it. Does that make Enoch scriptural? And if so, for whom?

Overall, then, the phenomenon of the NT writers' use of the Jewish Scriptures is a wide and diverse one, with numerous interpretative implications.

Example

The Use of Israel's Scriptures in Matthew 1–2

Even a cursory read of Matthew's birth narrative demonstrates its debt to the Jewish Scriptures. It opens with an extended genealogy whose framework of three units of fourteen generations (Matt 1.2–6; 1.7–11; 1.12–16) is shaped around Matthew's assessment of key elements within Israel's story—Abraham→David, David→Babylon deportation, Babylon deportation→Jesus. The next 'generation'—the seventh seven in terms of Matthew's prior counting (*ie* each fourteen equates to two batches of seven)—therefore becomes that inaugurated by/in Jesus, and the evangelist avowedly roots its origins and significance in Israel's story. From its very outset, Matthew's presentation of Jesus is located within the narrative of Israel's Scriptures, and the reader will be encouraged to make connections accordingly.[2]

Matthew's presentation of Jesus is located within the narrative of Israel's Scriptures

The subsequent narration of the events surrounding Jesus' birth reinforces, deepens even, this scriptural perspective (Matt 1.18–2.22). The narrative contains five explicit quotations which Matthew proposes are fulfilled in respect of Jesus' birth, with the fulfilment language a consistent thread across them all (Matt 1.23, 2.6, 2.15, 2.18, 2.23). This underscores the way in which—for Matthew—it is the incarnation that requires scriptural warrant. There is comparatively little fulfilment language in Matthew's account of Jesus' death—indeed it is only the death of Judas that so warrants that designation (Matt 27.9–10). To paraphrase 1 Cor 15.3, Matthew speaks of Jesus Christ *born* according to the Scriptures.

Whilst the volume of the Matthean fulfilment declaration is loud, close attention to its constituent parts still raises significant questions. In Matt 2.5–6, Matthew seemingly quotes Micah 5.2, but the cited text differs from that found in Micah itself. It is opposite, even, to the Micah original. Bethlehem has moved from being the *least* among the rulers of Judah to now becoming 'by no means' least among them. It could be that Matthew has faithfully reinterpreted the Micah text for his own purposes, bringing out its spirit rather than its letter; or it might be that Matthew has simply changed it to fit his own interpretative agenda. More positively, we might say that the NT writers felt they had the freedom to interpret the text in the light of Jesus Christ, and to bring forth its essence or purpose, even if that occasioned misquoting the text's original form. One assumes that Matthew's readers—or at least the well-informed amongst them—would have recognized the reversal and viewed this as permissible or legitimate.

The NT writers felt they had the freedom to interpret the text in the light of Jesus Christ

Matthew 2.5–6 is not the only instance of the evangelist's creativity. The final citation—'he will be called a Nazorean'—has no preceding scriptural text, at least not one in our known OT manuscripts, and this likewise creates potentially problematic questions (Matt 2.23). Can the refence to Nazorean be viewed as a mis-writing of Nazirite (compare Num 6.2)? Or is it the case that Matthew has merely 'created' an OT text for his own convenience? Or is the citation expected to have wider reference, to capture the essence of the whole prophetic tradition, rather than merely one specific text? Might it draw out the fundamental principle that the one who fulfils and personifies the expectations of Israel's prophets is a figure from Nazareth—the margins, so to speak—rather than from the centre, namely Jerusalem?

The first quotation (Matt 1.23) is more secure in terms of its textual source (*ie* Isa 7.14), though its interpretative implications are awash with theological significance. An angel appears to Joseph, alerting him to Mary's imminent conception, and telling him explicitly to name the child Jesus, because he will save his people from their sins (Matt 1.22–23). Such naming and justification echo the account of Israel's exodus, as Joshua / Jesus is the one who successfully leads Israel out of Egypt and into salvation in the Promised Land. The holy family likewise leave Egypt to return to the land of Israel (Matt 2.22–23), and Matthew can also find fulfilment in the need to place Jesus in Egypt—'out of Israel I have called my son' (Matt 2.15, citing Hos 11.1). Appearing to Joseph in a dream might also echo the dream-interpreter character of OT Joseph (compare also Matt 2.13, 2.19), particularly as—like the Joseph of Genesis—the family flee to Egypt to escape Herod's slaughter (Matt 2.13–15).

But even if the so-called Emmanuel prophecy / citation is textually secure, its significance warrants further OT investigation. Two points immediately come to mind. Drawing on the Isaianic source (Isa 7.14), Matthew uses the term *parthenos,* a Greek form that may be rendered as 'virgin,' and ideas around the Virgin Birth derive from this accordingly. However, there is no element of such matters in the Hebraic form, where the word *'almah* is essentially (just) a woman of young age. Isaiah 7.14 is a prophecy, uttered unto Ahaz, of God's (YHWH's) response to Judah's iniquity, and does not make any claim for a *virgin* birth. Matthew does not exploit the virgin birth in the rest of the gospel, and one might expect him to do so if it was a feature of the Isaianic fulfilment.

Secondly, why is there a second naming, particularly when the angel has already placed such stress on Jesus' naming and the salvation it thereby anticipates (Matt 1.21)? Jesus is also to be named *Emmanuel,* which in Hebrew literally means 'God with us' (Matt 1.23). This name is invariably heard today as a source of comfort or support, that God is present with and to humanity. But is that quite what Isaiah had in mind? If we look at the context of Isaiah 7–8, we might wish to nuance our perception of what 'Emmanuel' conveys. In Isa 7.13, the house of David is accused of wearying God, suggesting perhaps that the Emmanuel sign of 7.14 may be as much a warning as a positive. Furthermore, Isa 8.8 clarifies the Emmanuel nomenclature—Emmanuel is associated with the divine *judgment* of Assyria upon Judah. Emmanuel remains the very presence of YHWH, but such presence is double-edged, incorporating salvation *and* judgment. To reject the one who will save people from their sins is to invite the judgment of Emmanuel. The reader's response to Emmanuel is therefore critical and shapes the rest of the gospel account—will they embrace the salvation inaugurated by Jesus or will they face the judgment that accompanies any such rejection?[3]

In sum, Matthew 1–2 illustrates the value—the importance even—of attending to the scriptural connections found within the NT text, and that probing such connections yields significant interpretative consequences. To rephrase Hengel's soundbite, to know the NT *well* is to know more than *just* the NT itself.

2 Sources: What Scriptural Texts are Used and in Which Form?

How then do we take account of the use of the OT within NT texts? To what do we need to be alert? As we saw in the examples from Matthew 2, the *source* of the respective quotation potentially carries a significant explanatory burden, whether in terms of a change to the text of the citation, whether/how the context of the OT citation might impact upon the NT usage, or whether a source text even existed in the first place. A good first question to ask of any NT scriptural reference, therefore, is to ponder what its OT source might be, and what significance that has for its subsequent NT usage.

Considering the Source of an OT Citation

The term 'source' can, of course, pertain to several different—if related—concepts, but its primary reference is the (original) location of the cited text or idea, where it comes from, in effect. Scholars often use the German term *Vorlage* to denote or specify this original source. In many instances, identification of the *Vorlage* is a straightforward matter—or at least the book/chapter/verse is reasonably clear (and the footnotes in some English Bibles will normally indicate this, pointing the reader to the original OT source).

The quotation of Ps 110.1 in Heb 1.13 is a case in point. There is no other candidate for the source, particularly in respect of its distinctive imperative to sit at God's right hand. Appeals to Psalm 110 reappear frequently across the whole of the epistle, whether in terms of the right hand of God (Heb 8.1; 10.12) or the appeal to the order of Melchizedeck (Ps 110.4; compare Heb 5.6; 7.17). Various other NT texts cite Psalm 110 (*inter alia* Matt 22.44; Mark 12.36; Acts 2.34; 1 Cor 15.25), and indeed, it appears to be the most cited OT text in the NT. Such frequent appeal is perhaps unsurprising. The notion of a figure seated at YHWH's right hand could be theologically problematic within monotheistic understanding, and there is little sense that Psalm 110 was a go-to text within Jewish messianic expectation. However, for those seeking to make sense of Jesus Christ, and the worship of him as God, such positioning is ultimately most appropriate. One could see why a church trying to make sense of Jesus Christ would find grist for their theological mill in the psalm's claims. For the modern NT reader, recognizing that the citation comes from such a distinctive text as Psalm 110 enriches their interpretation of the NT text (and generates questions such as whether Ps 110.1b—'until I make your enemies your footstool'—is also on Hebrews' radar, as it is in Paul's [1 Cor

15.25]). In sum, identifying and knowing the source text has potential explanatory significance.

But such clarity or simplicity is not always the case when identifying a citation's *Vorlage*, and the attentive reader might well identify some ambiguity or variation in this regard. Sometimes the source of a quotation might look straightforward, but close attention suggests otherwise. For example, Luke 4.18–19 contains an explicit quotation of Isa 61.1–2, signalled by Jesus himself opening up and reading from the Isaiah scroll. The citation is placed at the outset of Jesus' ministry, offering something of a programmatic or manifesto statement for Jesus' ministry, a text that is fulfilled in the synagogue's hearing (Luke 4.21). However, a close reading / comparison of the respective texts reveals that Luke has omitted aspects of Isa 61.1–2 (the binding up of the broken-hearted or the announcement of the day of God's vengeance) that may not fit with Luke's purposes, whilst also substituting in material from Isa 58.6 (letting the oppressed go free). Luke can thus amend or reshape the source, or perhaps he even has a different source from the one with which we are familiar. Either way, paying attention to what is added to, or omitted from, Isa 61.1–2 generates insights as to why such amendment and variation has taken place.

Likewise, as we noted of Matt 2.23, sometimes the alleged citation's *Vorlage* is not obvious or rather does not seem to exist, at least not to our knowledge. Or sometimes, the alleged source does not quite seem to be the case. Take, for instance, the quotation with which Mark opens its gospel: the citation of a forthcoming messenger preparing the way, along with the associated admonition to make his path straight (Mark 1.2–3). Mark attributes the quotation to the prophet Isaiah but the first part of the citation (Mark 1.2) is not Isaianic (only the latter part is—Isa 40.3). Instead, it derives from either Exod 23.20,or, more likely, Mal 3.1, and hence the context and source of the Malachi aspect might also form part of Mark's exhortation, along with that of Isaiah 40. Some later manuscripts of Mark correct the reference to Isaiah—and instead render 'as is written in the prophets.' This can generate concern as to whether Mark was being deceitful or merely forgetful in terms of his scriptural citation. More likely, Isaiah emerges as Mark's overall primary conversation partner—hence the attribution—and the Malachi / Exodus reference gets subsumed within that.

Questions of source also extend to the specific text form cited by the NT author

Questions of source also extend to the specific *text form* cited by the NT author. The source of most English versions of the Old Testament is the so-called Leningrad Codex, the form of the Hebrew Bible known as the 'Masoretic Text' (MT)—so named after the scribes, the Masoretes, responsible for the preservation of the text's integrity and vocalization. But of course, the NT writers wrote in Greek, and hence there is an immediate linguistic difference so occasioned. Familiarity with Hebrew was dwindling, and Greek had become the *lingua franca*. Hence, the 'Bible' (*sic*) of the NT writers is more likely to have been those (Greek) texts found within the Old Greek or Septuagint (LXX) version(s) of Israel's Scriptures.

As Karen Jobes and Moses Silva rightly point out, 'Strictly speaking, there is no such thing as the Septuagint.'[4] Instead, there are a number of traditions or forms of the Greek scriptural text in circulation, and we can only speculate as to what is or was the original or definitive version. Moreover, there can be contrasting theological or textual perspectives found across and between traditions. Take Deut 32.4, for example, and the personification of God therein as a rock. The MT takes this perspective and is happy for God to be described with this metaphor. The LXX, however, is more reticent about such characterization and omits the rocky reference completely. This perhaps has implications for our reading of 1 Cor 10.1–13—a passage we will return to later—and Paul's contention that the rock which followed Israel in the wilderness and which brought forth water was Christ (1 Cor 10.4—a contention not made by Exodus!). Some commentators suggest that this is an allusion to Deut 32.4, and a reference to the rocky characterization of God therein, and that is certainly plausible bearing in mind how Deut 32.4 characterizes God the rock in terms of faithfulness. But equally, it means that Paul is appealing to a tradition found, as far as we know, only in Hebrew sources; as a Pharisee, he could likely read Hebrew too. Paul's primary 'source text' remains the LXX (Greek texts were simply more available and accessible), but this would be an example whereby account needs to be taken of a plurality of sources being available to a NT author.

Account needs to be taken of a plurality of sources being available to a NT author

What difference does this make in terms of assessing the NT author's usage of OT texts? How is it more than just a technical matter, and/or one that has implications for modern-day reading of NT texts? As a minimum, it recognizes that a plurality of textual sources existed in the first century, with different source options thus available. This does not mean that the NT writer necessarily chose the text form that suited them—it may be that they knew only one—but it at least opens up the possibility of differing interpretation, depending upon which form is used. Take, for example, the citation of Ps 40.6 in Heb 10.5–6, an integral element of Hebrews' discourse on the inefficacy of the sacrificial system. The MT version of Ps 40.6 reads, 'You have given me an open ear,' whereas Hebrews renders it as 'a body you have prepared for me,' suitably so in view of Christ's sacrificial offering of his own body. LXX manuscripts have the same (body) reading as Hebrews, and hence it may be that the author has actively chosen the LXX version to suit his expository purposes. Equally, though, the reverse may be the case; that is, Hebrews introduced the idea of 'body' into Ps 40.6 and subsequent scribes preserved that in Greek manuscripts of Psalm 40. Either way, addressing the OT source question has ramifications for the argument being made in the NT text, and it keeps us attentive to what motivates the author's source usage.

Secondly, it also draws out exactly what elements of an OT text get cited by a NT author and what do not. As we suggested above in respect of Luke 4's use of Isa 61.1–2, there is at least some selectivity in terms of Luke's appropriation of the material, and what it omits of Isa 61.1–2 might carry as much interpretative significance as what it includes. Parallel to this is the strange citation of Isa 53.12 in Luke 22.37, and the declaration that Jesus would be 'counted among the lawless.' Luke does not expand or exegete the citation, and the final clause of Isa 53.12 (compare 'he bore the sin of many, and made intercession for the transgressors') is not cited and at best echoes in the interpretative background. Instead, the fulfilment of the Isa 53.12 citation is tied to the need to have a sword (Luke 22.36–38), a strange connection bearing in mind that Isaiah 53 makes no mention of swords! Attending to the source of the quotation perhaps only complexifies the situation, but it at least opens up discussion on how / why Luke is using Isaiah 53 in respect of Jesus' death.

Attending to the source of an individual citation might also reveal a particular pattern across the whole of the NT text, and thus whether that pattern has explanatory significance. Recognition of the fact that Hebrews cites several times from the Song of Moses (Deut 32), for example, suggests a deliberate rhetorical strategy for the epistle, likely seeking to replicate the OT context of the Song, namely the leadership handover from Moses to Joshua at the threshold of entry into the Promised Land. Similarly, the attribution to Isaiah of the opening quotation of Mark 1.2–3 may point to Isaiah (particularly chapters 40–55) actually being a controlling narrative or template for Mark's portrayal of Jesus. Identifying the source of the quotation can help also inform as to why the citation is present in the first place, particularly if that is not immediately evident.

Identifying the source of the quotation may inform as to why the citation is present.

One final word on the notion of source. We drew attention earlier to 1 Cor 15.3 and the foundational, kerygmatic notion that Christ died according to the Scriptures. Paul gives no source for that contention, no quotation or citation in that regard. Why not, one might ask? Quite likely it is because there is not an obvious source text to which to appeal. Generally speaking, a crucified messiah was a contradiction in terms within Jewish understanding, and the challenge for the early church was precisely to find scriptural warrant for what appeared to be the inherent flaw of 'Christ crucified.' Perhaps the closest we can find to an individual source for 1 Cor 15.3 and its suffering / crucified Messiah is Dan 9.26 or Ps 89.50–51, but neither of these are cited within the NT. Hence in terms of the source for 1 Cor 15.3, we might say that it is an amalgam of scriptural texts, a plurality of sources that speak to the concept, rather than being merely a singular one.

Example

The Use of Amos at the Council of Jerusalem in Acts 15

Acts 15.1–29 relates the gathering of the so-called Council of Jerusalem, the assembly of the early church to assess the impact of Gentile believers becoming followers of the Way. What expectations would be asked of them? Would they be required to be circumcised and / or keep Torah (compare Acts 15.5)? First Peter (Acts 15.7–11), and then Barnabas and Paul (Act 15.12), report back on what God had been doing among Gentiles, and the Council is charged with discerning what might be the appropriate response.

It is James the Just who assumes the role as spokesperson or chair of the gathering. In his opening statement, James' primary justification for Gentile inclusion is the witness of Scripture, and that it is in accord with prophetic expectation (Acts 15.15). James's starting point—his fundamental premise—is Scripture, in accord with the posture of 1 Cor 15.3–4. This is intriguing, for Luke has already recorded Jesus himself querying distinguishing markers of Jewish identity (for example, the debate around table cleanliness—Luke 11.37–41), and what has taken place in the first half of Acts is commensurate with the Lucan anticipation of Gentile inclusion (compare Luke 2.32). It might seem natural for Luke's James to claim that the recounted events vindicate Jesus' credentials and / or that Jesus himself anticipated these things. However, that is not the case; it is Scripture that holds such authority, Scripture that is vindicated, Scripture that is ultimately proven.

James' primary justification for Gentile inclusion is the witness of Scripture

More significantly for our purposes, the text to which James appeals (and finds scriptural vindication) is the LXX form of Amos 9.11–12. In Jerusalem, in the 'Jewish' church, one might have expected James to appeal to the MT, particularly as he seems to be pronouncing the declaration as leader of the church there. However, James appeals to the *Septuagint* text form rather than the Masoretic one, and his choice (or that of Luke) is significant. Where the LXX form of the text is open to Gentile inclusion and anticipates a rebuilding of Israel, a process that enables other nations to seek YHWH, the Masoretic form takes the contrary position. Within Amos 9.11–12 MT, the rebuilding of David's booth—*ie* Israel—is not to enable the participation of the nations, but rather to facilitate Israel's ultimate *possession* of the nations. This appears to be the direct opposite of the LXX's testimony, and hence the two versions of Amos 9.11–12 espouse very different positions in respect of the fate of the nations. It is possible that the MT's notion of possession anticipates the eventual inclusion of the nations, thereby reducing the difference, but that need not be the case. Rather, Luke's citation of Amos simply exemplifies the textual pluriformity occasionally encountered in the first century. The Hebrew and Greek versions of Israel's Scriptures were self-standing traditions in their own right, rather than one being merely the translation of the other. Text forms varied, and the rendering of Amos 9.11–12 found within the LXX was the one Luke found more convivial for his purposes.

The extension of the gospel to Gentiles is, of course, thematic for Luke-Acts, and is anticipated by Luke's birth narrative, even if it awaits the second Lucan volume for it to come to fruition. At Jesus' presentation in the temple, Simeon pronounces that Jesus will be 'a light for revelation to the Gentiles' (Luke 2.32), a prophetic utterance that is, once again, sourced and premised on a direct quotation of Isaiah (Isa 42.6; 49.6). Simeon's Isaianic utterance reaches its next stage of fulfilment in James' proclamation of Amos, but Luke needs that proclamation to be sourced from the Greek tradition rather than the Masoretic one. The NT writers make choices about which scriptural sources they cite, and these choices have significant interpretative and theological implications.

3 Methods: How are the Scriptural Texts Used in the New Testament?

In the last chapter, we looked at the concept of sources, and the specific text(s) from which the NT writers sourced their scriptural appeal. We now turn to the related question of *how* they went about using those source texts—the methods and principles that may have informed this. We might distinguish two features in this regard. First, there is a question of means— *ie* what techniques are available to them? What other interpretative options are possible? What are the accepted parameters for utilizing a scriptural text in the first century CE? Secondly, and related to this, is the 'why so?'—why are certain methods or approaches adopted and/or what causes a NT author to read a scriptural text in a particular fashion? To these matters we now turn.

Contemporary Methods of Reading and Interpreting Scripture

We cannot overstress the fact that the NT writers participated in a pre-existing context of scriptural engagement and interpretation. Mapping their practice against that of their predecessors and contemporaries will likely reveal the distinctiveness of the NT approach(es). We are increasingly aware of different ways in which the Jewish Scriptures were being interpreted, whether in the Qumran Scrolls, or in the writings of other Jewish interpreters (such as Philo of Alexandria), or in the wider corpus of Second Temple Jewish literature (particularly those texts we know as the Pseudepigrapha). We also encounter a practice which later commentators have called 'Rewritten Bible,' namely the process by which the familiar narratives of the Jewish Scriptures were expanded, developed and reworked by contemporary scribes or groups. The text known as Jubilees, for example, is a re-writing of the Book of Genesis, together with some elements of Exodus, and expands and develops that text accordingly. Such textual reworking seems to have been both permissible and encouraged if/as it enabled the meaning(s) of a text to be unpacked for its readers. At the same time, this results in further textual fluidity, and opens up extra questions as to the NT author's scriptural source—what is *their* form of Genesis, for example? As such, we might say that the boundary between text and interpretation becomes blurred, or at least less distinct than in our modern conception.

One of the most apposite comparisons may be with the Qumran community, and the mode of interpretation found within the pesharim manuscripts found within the Dead Sea Scrolls. The word *pesher* means 'interpret' and denotes the form or genre of biblical interpretation characteristically found at Qumran. Many of the OT Prophets have pesharim composed on them (Nahum, Zephaniah, Isaiah). What is interesting, though, is that the psalms were also the object of *pesher* interpretation, and were thus perceived as having some prophetic, as well as liturgical, dimension. Hence the NT writers were not the first to see the psalms as anticipating some kind of fulfilment. They were elsewhere regarded as such.

> **Overall, the Pesharim apply a fulfilment dimension to the scriptural texts**

The standard pesharim format is the citation of the biblical verse and then the heading *'Interpreted'*—the key term *pesher*, the *sine qua non* of the exegetical mode. The pesherist's interpretation then follows, stating what the text means and how it is being fulfilled. The practice looks something like our modern-day verse-by-verse commentary, at least in format. Overall, the pesharim apply a fulfilment dimension to the scriptural texts; things predicted once are now taking place in their time. The community generally conceive of Hebrew prophecy as predictive, rather than admonitory, and such prophetic anticipation plays out in the life and experience of the community. Such perception is not too different from the NT writers' approach of (re-)reading biblical texts in the light of their own experience, and particularly the experience of Jesus Christ.

The most studied pesher document is the Habakkuk pesher, mainly because it is the one best preserved, but also because of the comparative insights it yields. Consider the importance of Hab 2.4 to Paul, and the apostle's discussion of the relationship between righteousness and living by faith, much of which derives from Paul's reading of the Habakkuk text (compare Rom 1.17; Gal 3.11–12). How that text was used / understood by the Qumran community offers a contemporary comparison to that of Paul (and also to Hebrews, which offers another take on the Hab 2.4 quotation—Heb 10.38). For example, does the righteous person live by their own exercise of faith, or it is the outcome of Christ's own manifest faithfulness? The pesherist proposes that the text addresses the deliverance of those who put their faith in the Teacher of Righteousness (a primary figure within the Qumran community). Whilst the object of such faith is different from that outlined by Paul, one can at least see some parallels with Paul's focus on the exercise of faith in a particular figure and the capacity to read the Habakkuk text in the light of the reader's experience.

Why Read Scripture in a Particular Way?

Discussion of matters of technique then lead us to *why* a NT author chooses to use a particular exegetical lens and / or why they end up reading a scriptural text in a particular way. What motivates their specific reading lens and / or how is it different from that of their peers? How might it be shaped, for example, by / to the context to which the NT text is addressed? And how might it be influenced by christological insights or perspectives?

Let us take the apostle Paul as a case in point, and particularly his distinctive—or rather distinct—reading of Gen 15.6. Paul uses its short, terse statement ('Abram believed the LORD, and he credited it to him as righteousness') in several key episodes in his letters (Rom 4.3; Gal 3.6), and the *pisteuo* (believe) language resonates with the *pistis* (faith / faithfulness) imagery (drawn from the same lexical root) that Paul addresses through the Hab 2.4 citation and its appeal to justification by faith / faithfulness. That is, how does Paul understand Gen 15.6 and what it meant for Abram to believe / articulate faith in God? And how does this understanding compare to other interpreters contemporary with Paul and their reading of the same Genesis text?

In the epistle of James, the same text—Gen 15.6—is cited (Jas 2.23), and approvingly so. Abraham is termed a friend of God because of his belief. But for James, it is the offering of Isaac, the *Akedah*, that ultimately demonstrates the fulfilment of Gen 15.6. Even though the sacrifice technically does not happen, Abraham's intent to complete it effectively makes it happen, and it becomes the ultimate manifestation of Abraham's faithfulness. James stands very much in a tradition of other Second Temple interpreters in arriving at that assessment. Philo and others also find it to be the ultimate way in which Abraham's faithfulness is attested. James' position is the standard or consensus one.

Paul ends up utilizing the text in contrasting fashion to that of James et al

However, Paul ends up utilizing the text in contrasting fashion to that of James *et al*. Paul has read the Scripture differently, or arrived at an alternative interpretation of Gen 15.6 to that of James. Abraham's belief or faith is ultimately or manifestly displayed not in the offering of Isaac—indeed, Paul exhibits relatively little interest in that scriptural episode. Instead, it is the simple act of belief / faith announced by Genesis 15 that manifests the ultimate demonstration of Abraham's faithfulness—Abraham *believed* God and it was credited to him as righteousness. Hence, within the NT testimony, we have two contrasting assessments of the evidencing or outworking of Abraham's faith, and this has led—at least on the surface—to contrasting positions on the grounds for justification, whether by action or by faith. Two different NT writers read the same scriptural text in two very different ways.

Something therefore must have occasioned Paul to read differently to his peers, to interpret Gen 15.6 (as opposed to Genesis 22) as the ultimate embodiment of Abraham's faithfulness. Why so? There are a number of answers to that question, of course, but at the very least, it suggests that texts are being (re)-read in the light of the experience of Jesus Christ and/or the Christ event. That is, the engagement with Christ generates new or different ways of interpreting the Scriptures, and such rereading can impact significantly on the life of faith. We might term this as reading christologically—the meaning of the text evolves or develops, maybe changes even, as the reader reflects on the encounter with the crucified and risen Christ.

Example

The Use of the Wilderness Narratives in 1 Corinthians 10.1-13

What might this look like in practice? Let us take 1 Cor 10.1–13 as an illustrative example of how Paul has appropriated a familiar text and reread it christologically, drawing explicit connection between the wilderness generation and the presenting issues facing his Corinthian audience. It is also a case study of the kind of techniques Paul applies to the scriptural text. First Corinthians 10.1–13 is one of—if not the—longest scripturally-sourced retellings in the Pauline epistolary corpus, and manifests an array of scriptural images, citations and motifs. Paul recounts the story of Israel's exodus journey (interestingly so for the Gentile audience in Corinth—it suggests that they would have been generally familiar with the story), and the broad elements of the narrative remain mostly unchanged and/or consistent—the pillar of cloud (1 Cor 10.1; Exod 13.21–22), the feeding of manna (1 Cor 10.3; Exod 16.31–35), the rock that yielded water (1 Cor 10.4; Exod 17.1–7) and the climactic golden calf incident (1 Cor 10.7; Exod 32.1–6).

There are key points of difference or novelty in Paul's retelling

But at the same time, there are key points of difference or novelty in Paul's retelling. Elements of the narrative are reworked or re-interpreted in the light of Paul's experience of Jesus Christ. First, in a significant hermeneutical shift Paul explicitly identifies Israel as the ancestors of the Corinthian church (1 Cor 10.1): in some sense, the experience of wilderness Israel becomes that of (Gentile) Christian Corinth. Secondly, and linked to this, Paul reads Israel's wilderness experiences as having occurred 'for us' (1 Cor 10.6), and composed/recorded for the Corinthians' benefit (1 Cor 10.11). They have heuristic value for Paul's contemporary readers as well as for Israel itself. Thirdly, aspects of the narrative get re-worked or amended to fit the Corinthian context or situation. The wilderness manna was heavenly (Exod 16.4–25), and likewise the drink has become spiritual in Paul's reworking (Exod 17.6). The distinction is not a huge one, and it is not contrary to the Exodus version, but equally the spiritual language is shaped by the epistolary context and occasion, and the Corinthians' misunderstanding of spirituality (compare 1 Cor 2.13). Paul wants his audience to learn from the experience of the wilderness generation—the events have happened for *their* benefit—and the account is Christianized as such.

Perhaps the most striking element of Paul's re-narration is his declaration that the rock is *Christ*, an avowedly christological (and christocentric?) addition to the Exodus script, and one that most likely derives from Paul himself as he seeks—within 1 Corinthians—to address the stumbling block of Christ crucified. As noted above, Paul's association of the rock with Christ may have roots in Deut 32.4, or even Ps 95.1, but even there, it is *God*—rather than Christ—that is so characterized, and thus there is a distinct novelty to Paul's retelling. But at the same time, this need not rule out the influence of other Jewish exegetical practice, and commends the approach discussed above which is attentive to other Second Temple approaches and what comparative insight they might so yield. Philo, for example, describes the exodus well/rock as a source of 'incomparable wisdom' (*Ebr.* 112), and partaking from the well/rock equated to partaking of the very wisdom of God.[5] The rock is God—rather than Christ—but its divine personification is not *too* different from Paul's attribution.

Pedagogical principles undergird Paul's application of the text, as he presents four scenarios drawn from the wilderness narratives from which the Corinthians might learn (1 Cor 10.6). In each warning (or at least the latter three), the wilderness generation's error is outlined, and their resultant punishment or fate then set forth. Once again, the wilderness narrative matters as much for the contemporary reader as for the Israelite participants, perhaps even more so (compare 1 Cor 10.6). Both the present moment *and* the 'original' one drive Paul's analysis.

4 Presenting Issues

What then are the presenting issues in respect of the use of the OT in the NT? What questions arise and what sort of matters should contemporary interpreters be attentive to when working with the biblical text? I explore three particular issues in this regard.

How Do We Know That the OT is Being Utilized?

In many instances, the presence of an OT citation is explicitly signalled. In the case of a formal quotation, there will normally be some type of introductory formula to demarcate the cited text. At other times, the citation might not be a direct quotation, but instead a phrase or image, and one sufficiently familiar for the audience to make the OT connection. Increasingly, though, we are recognizing more subtle connections to the OT; they are less explicit and often amount to just one or two words. Such connections, or echoes as they are commonly known, can be explanatorily significant, but equally it can be a moot point as to whether they genuinely exist. That is, on what basis does the reader identify such an echo, and/or adjudicate on its genuineness?

In his work on Pauline echoes, Richard Hays introduces seven tests or criteria by which one might evidence or assess the existence of a scriptural echo:[6]

- *Availability*: was the proposed source text available to the author and/or readers?
- *Volume*: how many points of connection are there? How loud is the mooted echo?
- *Recurrence*: does the author make similar appeal elsewhere?
- *Thematic coherence*: how does the echo accord with the overall argument being made?
- *Historical plausibility*: could the readers have reasonably understood or appropriated the echo?
- *History of interpretation*: have other subsequent interpreters heard the echo?
- *Satisfaction*: does the reading make sense—does it yield explanatory power?

Subsequent commentators have sought to nuance or critique these criteria, or questioned whether one can even assess the existence of a literary echo by what can sound like more scientific means. But we might say that these criteria offer a useful starting point for assessing the existence or otherwise of an allusion or echo—they are at least good questions to ask of the suggested OT link. They might, for example, suggest that the reference to the poisonous capacity of the tongue in Jas 3.8 has resonances of Gen 3.1–5 and the serpent's crafty tongue, particularly in view of the species-naming language of Jas 3.7 (compare Gen 2.19–20). Equally, they might rein in enthusiasm as to an alleged echo of Song 4.13–14 in John 12.3—different readers will come to different conclusions. What weighting one gives to each criterion will vary from reader to reader, of course, as will the actual level of pre-existing knowledge and awareness of that reader. Echoes of familiar narratives such as the Exodus might be more persuasive than those of more obscure voices within, say, the Minor Prophets corpus.

The assessment of an echo's existence ultimately remains a subjective exercise

The assessment of an echo's existence ultimately remains a subjective exercise, an art rather than a science, and it is the reader who ultimately makes the connection. As such, we might suggest a rule of thumb, namely that the satisfaction criterion perhaps carries the most significance—that is, does the mooted allusion/echo make sense? Put simply, does it really *work* and make an interpretative difference?

What 'Extra' Context Comes with the OT Citation?

Assuming there is an allusion or reference to the OT, this then invites the question of how much of its wider or original context might carry over. Take a non-biblical instance, for example. The saying 'To be or not to be, that is the question' has become something of a stock phrase in English and may be used with no reference to its original (Shakespearean) context. At the same time, of course, the phrase draws from Hamlet and has some functionality or meaning associated with it at that point, and it is entirely possible that such meaning is carried over into whatever new context in which it is being used.

Such a perspective assumes that the author of the text is ultimately responsible for the mooted OT connection—the allusion is 'intended' in that sense. However, assessing the impact or resonance of an OT text's context also needs to take account of the audience's awareness of that image/context. For example, for many English people, mention of the year 1966 carries with it the imagery and memory of England winning the World Cup. For those who share that memory or connection, one has only to mention the year and the football imagery is rhetorically carried over with it, and fruitfully so. But the transfer only makes sense for those who know of the link and can make the connection. For those unaware of the association, 1966 is a calendar year and nothing else.

One might say the same of NT echoes or allusions to an OT text; what rhetorical effect would a quotation have for the audience? How much contextual transfer is there, for example, in Paul's somewhat opaque quotation of Deut 25.4 regarding the muzzling of an ox (1 Cor 9.9)? What—if anything—would the Gentile Corinthians have made of that rather obscure citation? Or what about the phrase 'abomination that makes desolate' (Dan 11.31), the image used, we think, in respect of Antiochus Epiphanes' pollution of the temple? This becomes a significant image in Jewish minds, encapsulating the profound sacrilegious desecration of the temple. It embodied the very essence of polluting the temple. It seems likely then that Mark 13.14's reference to the 'desolating sacrilege' both anticipates the Romans' destruction of the temple and invites the reader to hear this against the backdrop of Antiochus' actions. Mark's audience would need to know of Dan 11.31, of course, but the event is a prominent one in Second Temple thinking, and more significantly, Mark's 'let the reader understand' seems to specifically invite the contextual association (Mark 13.14).

There are some instances when invoking the wider context is necessary for the citation or allusion to work, or to have any bite. Consider our earlier discussion on 1 Corinthians 10. For the warning of 1 Cor 10.7 against idolatry to have any force, for the quotation of Exod 32.6 therein to have any effect, it requires the Corinthians to possess some knowledge of the wider context of the quotation and the accompanying narrative of the golden calf, including the accompanying consumption of food and drink sacrificed to idols (Exod 32.5–6). As such, Israel's rising to 'play' (1 Cor 10.7) and their accompanying idolatrous behaviour (rather than the actual building of the golden calf) becomes for Paul the scriptural precedent or warning Paul seeks to levy against the Corinthians. Francis Watson captures this as follows:

> Paul's warning against idolatry requires the reader to recognize the context of the passage cited in the story of the golden calf. Only a knowledge of the original context can fill the gap between a warning against idolatry and a scriptural text that, apart from its context, merely seems to speak of some unspecified festive occasion. Here at least, the reader's knowledge of the original context is indispensable.[7]

To put it another way, the context of the quotation and the context of the Corinthians are mutually informing. Paul's reading of the golden calf incident is shaped by his awareness of idolatrous behaviour at Corinth, but equally the (full) context of the Exodus narrative is brought to bear on his warning to Corinth. First Corinthians 10 is best understood when both situational narratives—the golden calf *and* Corinth—are put into mutual conversation.

What About the OT Context—Can it Change?

When an OT text is cited or referenced in the NT, it assumes a *new* context. This raises a further question for us—can the meaning of an OT text change or develop when it is used by a NT author? Specifically, must its usage—and meaning—necessarily be consistent with the OT precedent, or can it instead progress or evolve? Or can it even change and do something quite *different* from its prior usage?

At the very least, something changes in / with the OT text when the NT author references it. Because the cited text assumes a different context, it is necessarily invested with new or fresh meaning, and with meaning that might seem inconsistent with the prior OT context. But at the same time, to restrict the interpretation of the prior Scripture to merely one sense or understanding is itself problematic. OT authorial intent does not imply a singularity of meaning. Even within its original context, the scriptural text will be understood differently by different readers.

Hence the assessment of if / how the context of an OT citation operates will vary from reader to reader, and from text to text. There will likely be both continuity *and* change. Take the Letter to the Hebrews, for example. On the one hand, the epistle's anonymous writer stresses the novelty of the new covenant / testament—there is something inherently *de novo* to it, something that has rendered the old one obsolete (Heb 8.13). But on the other hand, the case for such novelty is made by appeal to Jer 31.31–34—it is a *self-attested* inadequacy or inefficacy of the OT. Hence there is both continuity *and* change, both consistency *and* discontinuity, and this encourages us to be attentive to the original context of OT usage / citation whilst also being alert to how it might be reread—or read differently—in a NT milieu.

Example

Scriptural Usage in Mark 14.62

Let us consider an example to test out some of these continuity / change questions, and the degree to which the OT context might remain operative in the NT location. Take the example of Jesus' trial and defence before the high priest in the Gospel of Mark (Mark 14.53–65). Various accusations are made against Jesus, and the narrative climaxes with Jesus questioned as to his identity, and specifically the direct question as to his messianic role (Mark 14.61). Jesus responds in positive terms, in what appears to be the ultimate moment of revelation (Mark 14.62). Where previously in the gospel his messianic status had invited silence, the tables are now turned, and Jesus authoritatively claims to be the Messiah. Such revelation is accompanied by a declaration which draws on a combination of two texts. Jesus claims to be both Daniel's Son of Man, the one coming on the clouds of heaven (Dan 7.13), and the one who sits at YHWH's right hand (Ps 110.1). There cannot be a much higher claim, but it is one whose weight is sustained by scriptural allusion.

The question then becomes as to how much of the respective Daniel 7 or Psalm 110 discourses continue to be operative in Jesus' statement. Does Jesus' Son of Man identification derive from the discourse of the one like a human being who is that mystical, other figure in the Daniel 7 portrayal? Similarly, the one who sits at YHWH's right hand (Ps 110.1) is also the one who is heralded as an eternal priest in the order of Melchizedek (Ps 110.4). Is Jesus claiming that priestly identity for himself, a stunning declaration before his high-priestly interrogator? If so, Jesus claims that his priesthood is eternal whereas that of the affronted high priest is only temporary, and implicitly deficient.

Now, it is a moot point as to how much of Daniel 7 or Psalm 110 is carried over into Mark 14. Mark's appeal to the two texts may be no more than an exhortatory appeal that carries no further contextual or interpretative insight. Similarly, if aspects do carry over, it may be that there are points of difference and contrast when effective in the new location. Neither Melchizedeck nor Jesus are *high* priests—unlike Jesus' interlocutor—so if there is some wider application of Ps 110.4 in Mark 14.62, then there is at least some effective variation from the original psalm form. But the example reveals at least the *possibility* of this, and demonstrates the interpretative options that probing the context of a text generates.

5 Concluding Thoughts

What more, then, shall we say (compare Heb 11.32)? This question was posed by one NT author for whom both the reflection on Jesus Christ and the exhortation to ongoing faithfulness derived from extended scriptural citation and reflection.

On the one hand, we have only started to discuss matters pertaining to the NT's use of Israel's Scriptures, and might expand further on questions of source, method and context. We might also want to say more about *over*-assessing links to the OT—how do we avoid overstating them and escape potential 'parallelomania'?[8] We might even comment on how the Old Testament texts are already performing an internal, interpretive task; that is, the Hebrew Bible is first its own interpreter, before the NT writers or other interpreters engage with it. And when attending to the NT writers' use of the OT in our preaching or in our Bible studies, there may well be less OT awareness on the part of our contemporary audience. Not every OT connection will be obvious to every NT reader.

But on the other hand, we have drawn out a number of features of the NT's use of the OT which might inform our reading of the biblical text. Quite simply, the NT writers were rooted in Israel's Scriptures, and their narration, discussion and reflection drew extensively on those Scriptures. Some summary observations might therefore be made:

- Broadly speaking, the NT authors read the OT in the light of the Christ event, and mediated by their faith in Jesus Christ. This generated a significant element of what we might term 'reading backwards,' namely reading Jesus Christ into the text of the Jewish Scriptures in ways that yielded some surprising claims. The fourth gospel, for example, avers that Moses specifically wrote about Jesus (John 5.46), or Hebrews ventures that Moses suffered abuse for Christ whilst in Egypt (Heb 11.26). But equally their scriptural reading might operate forwards too, with Christ understood as the *telos* or goal of the Law (Rom 10.4). Either way, their christological lens is the focal interpretive one.
- This means that differences emerge between how respective NT interpreters read Israel's Scriptures—and reminds us that there is

not just one 'correct' meaning to an OT text. There is a plurality of OT textual meaning, and the NT writers' varying usage of Israel's Scriptures testifies to this.

- Therefore, just because the NT author has read an OT text in a particular fashion, it need not mean that that is the only—or even the best—way to read it. But their reading can be helpful nonetheless; the NT authors enable us to understand the OT better, to recognize and assess the various interpretative options an OT text might (or might not) yield. We are encouraged to engage with the OT for ourselves and to make sense of it in our own context, just as the NT authors themselves did in the light of Jesus Christ.
- And when assessing how a NT author utilises an OT text, we will want to be attentive to textual fluidity—to the source of the citation and to its wider context. Asking why and how the OT is being used will be interpretatively fruitful for us as modern readers of both Testaments.

I hope that the preceding discussion has at least flagged the value of following the NT writers' lead in considering how they used Israel's Scriptures to articulate the significance of Jesus' life, death and resurrection. The exercise also reminds us that Israel's Scriptures are Christian Scripture too, and as such, they contribute to the life and faith of disciples of Jesus Christ.

For Further Reading

D M Allen, 'Introduction: The Study of the Use of the Old Testament in the New,' *Journal for the Study of the New Testament* 38 (2015) pp 3–16.

S Docherty, 'New Testament Scriptural Interpretation in Its Early Jewish Context,' *Novum Testamentum* 57 (2015) pp 1–19.

R Hays, *Echoes of Scripture in the Letters of Paul* (New Haven, CT: Yale University Press, 1989).

R B Hays, *Echoes of Scripture in the Gospels* (Waco, TX: Baylor University Press, 2016).

K H Jobes and M Silva, *Invitation to the Septuagint* (Grand Rapids, MI: Baker Academic, 2000).

S Moyise, *Was the Birth of Jesus According to Scripture?* (London: SPCK, 2013).

S Moyise, *Evoking Scripture: Seeing the Old Testament in the New* (London: T and T Clark, 2008).

L Novakovic, 'The Scriptures and Scriptural Interpretation' pp 85–101 in J B Green and LM McDonald (eds), *The World of the New Testament: Cultural, Social, and Historical Contexts* (Grand Rapids, MI: Baker Academic, 2013).

Notes

1 The term 'Old Testament' can be problematic and imply that such texts are redundant and silenced, which is precisely *not* how they are utilized by the NT writers. Hence other terms such as 'Israel's Scriptures' might also be used for that corpus of texts. At the same time, it remains a familiar designation for most readers and it is, of course, a term used by one NT author (Heb 8.13).

2 See further S Moyise, *Was the Birth of Jesus According to Scripture?* (London: SPCK, 2013).

3 R E Watts, 'Immanuel: Virgin Birth Proof Text or Programmatic Warning of Things to Come (Isa 7.14 in Matt. 1.23)?' in C A Evans (ed), *From Prophecy to Testament: The Function of the Old Testament in the New* (Peabody, MA: Hendrickson, 2004) pp 92–113.

4 K H Jobes and M Silva, *Invitation to the Septuagint* (Grand Rapids, MI: Baker Academic, 2000) p 30.

5 *Ebr* is the abbreviation for Philo's work *De ebrietate*—'On Drunkenness'—in which he explores Moses' and the Law's depiction of wine and the resultant implications of drinking it.

6 R Hays, *Echoes of Scripture in the Letters of Paul* (New Haven, CT: Yale University Press, 1989). See also R B Hays, *Echoes of Scripture in the Gospels* (Waco, TX: Baylor University Press, 2016).

7 F Watson, 'Scripture in Pauline Theology: How Far Down Does It Go?' *Journal of Theological Interpretation* 2 (2008) p 187.

8 Compare S Sandmel, 'Parallelomania,' *Journal of Biblical Literature* 81 (1962) pp 1–13. Sandmel coined the phrase as a cautionary note. For Sandmel, it manifested an 'extravagance among scholars which first overdoes the supposed similarity in passages and then proceeds to describe source and derivation as if implying literary connection flowing *in an inevitable or predetermined direction*' (emphasis added).